Great philosophical questions sometimes tak s
of as "ordinary" in a human's life is anything
Michael Burkard or Ralph Angel, these poems
humble origins of small events on mind-waves ....ebral at
the same time as being very deeply felt, nearly sentimental; they captivate the mind as
well as hear and reading them sends me on my own inner journey through time and
space and all the far or nearly forgotten moments of my own ordinary life.
–Kazim Ali, author of *Northern Light: Power, Land, and the Memory of Water*

The continuously solid knit between lines keeps the reader of *(no subject)* somewhat
breathless. The nouns are bathed in the luminous light of the everyday and the
landscape underneath the poetry rolls along in time with its cosmic american music.
"I exercise echo beyond the neighbor's pastel stucco and am similarly peeled back
by the sun." I felt a slight sonnet-like cradling at work in this book. In fact, these
perfectly weighted orchestrations are still dripping down the highways of my mind.
There are goodbyes lingering at every corner and miniature librettos performed
under heartbroken streetlight. The mood and phrasing pull equally hard to the point
that I'm not sure which parts are magic and which are sleight of hand. I only know
that I want back into this fading, crystalline world immediately.
–Cedar Sigo, author of *All This Time*

In these terse lyric meditations on the lightness of modern being, poems that veer
toward and shy away from epigrammatic certainty, Peter Burghardt reports on what
it means to embrace an ethos of responsibility without congealing into the fixtures
of ideology ("you can't choose something into truth,/ like you can into concept").
The trappings are real, from epistemological pathos ("You got old enough to recall
the shape/ of what you couldn't remember") to existential dread ("a house is a
special kind of box I spend/ my time in though I guess what adds up/ is always some
kind of container/ punctuated by the vastness/ of the packaging."). And Burghardt,
like many of us, is not immune to the allure of "online retail therapy" ("even though
I'm running out of want/ the want waits for me"). Still, no subject offers its readers
the real possibility of a future inasmuch as "The hope of a moment/...stands apart
from its birth." And that hope is inseparable from Burghardt's reminder that "What
was once destroyed/ is green today."
–Tyrone Williams, author of *As iZ*

(no subject)

Cover art by Marion Kryczka

Interior typeface: Garamond and Futura

Cover design by Peter Burghardt and
Interior design by Laura Joakimson

Library of Congress Cataloging-in-Publication Data

Names: Burghardt, Peter, 1984- author.
Title: (no subject) / Peter Burghardt.
Description: Oakland, California : Omnidawn Publishing, 2022. | Summary:
"The poems of (no subject) are an investigation of the personal
everyday. The title for the book and the poems contained within are
derived from the default subject line of a subjectless email. The books'
composition was informed by this idea of the quickly written subjectless
email, as the author would clear small periods of time to write and
record the observations and thoughts around himself at that moment, then
send it to himself for future refinement. In this way, the book takes
the shape of an impressionistic 21st-century diary, often reflecting on
themes of anxiety about the future and the situation of the present. As
these moments compound, the line between the present, past, and future
is blurred in the speaker's sense of self and memory. Driven by a
speaker who is nearly hermetically sealed in their private world, the
voice becomes a frame and eventual filter for the accumulations of their
immediate reality. Through a reserved staccato diction that swears
itself to the syllable, these ostensibly subjectless poems derive their
meaning through the tension between narrative and emotional resonances.
As such, (no subject) plumbs its depths in search of the big little
feelings transmitted by fatherhood, the fusion of time and space,
loneliness, resilience, and wonder"-- Provided by publisher.

Identifiers: LCCN 2022036098 | ISBN 9781632431080 (trade paperback)
Subjects: LCGFT: Poetry.
Classification: LCC PS3602.U748 N6 2022 | DDC 811/.6--dc23/eng/20220801
LC record available at https://lccn.loc.gov/2022036098

Published by Omnidawn Publishing, Oakland, California
www.omnidawn.com   (510) 237-5472
10 9 8 7 6 5 4 3 2 1
ISBN: 978-1-63243-108-0

(no subject)

Peter Burghardt

OMNIDAWN PUBLISHING
OAKLAND, CALIFORNIA
2022

Contents

(no subject)

You got old enough to recall the shape
of what you couldn't remember. When have I not
slept with my bed pressed to the wall?
Any perforation is torn
by the benefit of space between matter.
Expressing this to you, the root of my palm
moves in space to what I perceive
as an up-facing position. I am driving stick
across Atlanta limits. It's never easy to see
a house's number when you are looking
from the street, but somehow I am at home.
Here, there is a stake in the ground from which a line
leads to a collar. It's called a run and it rattles in the wind.
Continuosity is word I just made up and time
will not undo that. Nothing is ever undone
but one time I fell in a hole in the tall grass
of my front yard. I showed you where it was
and you had me answer how far down it goes. I said
I'm glad it's not deeper. I am wearing my boots again
and intend to have them resoled. The baby is nearly ready
for his first pair.

(no subject)

It took long so mystic becomes
streetlights where day used to begin.
A bird on the fence is banded.
Elsewhere, notness grows into you.
Washing my neck in the dark
I said I'd see no nothing
but meant I'm with the mud
and can neither walk inside nor step in it.
Imagine it's like what you beg for
when you shouldn't
mix insomnia with your abyss.
You tell yourself you'll pay for it
we're always paying
for what we thought
would be inheritance
though the mail still comes
on Saturdays. Our neighbor is thinking
of slaughtering his rooster.

(no subject)

I stand at Safeway wrapped
in the manner one assumes
when shopping alone
peering into passing carts
to see how much soda is loaded
on sale so weird I'd have thought
this self would not buy it
but it's easy for the holidays
just becomes an aperture of the body's craving
which enlarges like almost any fear
to be in want of what isn't restocked
sitting at home eating dinner with the lights off
another IRS letter arrived today, sixty more
dollars gone before I'm gone
to drink at G and V's
engagement party returning to
having left the lights on
knowing I'm about to hold
really honest conversation
with my dog.

(no subject)

People across the world settle in extremes.
Places where the ground is so hot you need
double-layered leather-lined shoes, or where
if you get drunk enough, you'll freeze to death.
The best technology sent to Mars isn't meant to return.
An architect says there is not a single building
that will never collapse. He says, on earth bridges
are what last the longest holding ruin in the world
until there is supernova. Which isn't to say it's a bad thing.
It's not like I can change the channel anyhow.
As an American, the camera is always on.
I waste too much time trying to figure out how I look.
The best trend is always a change or a return, settling
into reruns and knowing what they're not.
But didn't I realize that? Expansion isn't limitless,
and you can't choose something into truth,
like you can into concept.

(no subject)

My window is glazed by the great chime of the rain
as if an ask for anything outside may be a garden pathway
to the mind's diaristic briar patch which is to say the world
might end and I'm shopping for bassinets while being reminded
that optimism is a recital in three acts though the first is over
I find I still need to be alone inside less in my favorite season
which barely registers inside this coworking office
each day wrinkling my impression of the last
I wish I'd have learned to play piano
always had one but never got it tuned, too late now
to sleep which is one of the body's crueler hiccups and how
I learned to stop worrying and love coffee
now three cups a day, though like how my grandpa named his boat
What's Next before it sank, the future is a language
I don't understand.

(no subject)

The sky is bleeding over the shell of our tremulous vessel.
A correspondence with the land develops almost unnoticeably.
Paranoia. That we might be found is apparently enough.
A contemporary narrative collects its scattered pieces.
This human ilk is invasive. Our brains no longer beautiful
with thoughts cancerous and counterbalanceless.
Twenty species of birds pass our geometric thrum,
some throttled in midair. Our destruction glides on a bridge
of invisible heft taking for granted the poisonous incantations
spilled intentionally or not. If there is an alternative get me some
obsidian. Get me some idol. I've always had falling dreams
and thought that was a pessimistic trait. There is also immortality
in between the start and the stop.

(no subject)

Each hour wounds, the last
one kills. Inscribed on the sundial where
I sit in someone else's garden listening
to three kittens patter their stubby
legs in the planting soil, not yet
a year old but already practically cats
their kibble causing flies to flick
their filth around. The landlords
aren't happy about the mess
but they love the company.
The sun today is too much for the succulents
and tomatoes N planted. A text
arrives but the data won't load.
I feel I need to sit and think deeper
about my five-year plan which is
a joke I don't know how to finish.

(no subject)

We arrive in the early evening.
What we've come to expect
is more casual after time together.
Good behavior, a cumulative cadence.
Playing tag at dinner, one of our most exciting
things to do. When the night-birds come
to peck bugs, we move to the patio and watch.
As if I weren't too private already, I've learned
to rumor in the shade of my beer bottle.
Not a problem, situational. I rise, I walk.
Relaxation is opened by the natural dim.
We lie in a hammock out by the beasts' extreme melody.
Tomorrow I'll tour you the town. Put on wind
for my cousins. Out here, we're almost encouraged
to exist. There's even a television
built into the bathroom mirror.

(no subject)

We shouldn't have done that last glass.
Its rippling similar to what you see in movies.
When UFOs touch down their earthly mark
imprints this late evening with lights
all off. Bugs coming in, incandescence stripped
to bare threshold. Hold it in your mind but don't
say what's really matter, just as with any plot
you think you're smarter than.

(no subject)

The "I'm sorry" sunk into the way
we've been thinking with our crystal glassware
that's been cupboarded. One goblet for me
and another nighttime
without sleep's syrup.
Small shudders. Sounds
healthier than it is. I curl
with a new headphone
designed for canceling.
An expensive buoy
in this living room's riptide
that can't kill me.

(no subject)

Elsewhere, another noisemaker
became taxpayer footnote.
Anyone eyeballs themselves.
Teenager bedroom blackout
highlights ponytail, watermarked
into tenderfoot pinup.
Meanwhile, newsboy outputs
timesaving endgame. Eardrum
eavesdrops. Peacekeeper's handgun standoff
targets tenfold schoolteachers.
Shoreline sunups everyday.
Wingspan's wristwatch pawnbroker,
songbird housewife. Witchcraft therefore
outfoxes copywriter understanding.
Playthings herein earthquake together.
Forget backbone, faraway hometown
moreover, somehow standup.
Inside today, grasshopper
footprints thunderstorm allover.

(no subject)

Singing karaoke at Ben & Nick's
I forewent Wicked Games
my comfortable standby
because my wife hates that song
and after the Estrella Specials
I can't recall what I settled on.
I'm lying in bed now, the morning after
feeling the regret of choice I didn't make
to try something new, as I'm stuck
in my pajamas, too tucked in to move.
I'm not hungry anyhow.
Last night I dreamed about the last election
waiting in a line that never seems to move,
miles long as my mom calls to tell me
Reagan was elected the very day
I was born though she's wrong
like some b film apocalypse
it was the day after.

(no subject)

I'm asking for your help. You will hear me best
if you walk outside to where the street-sign drips
with the din of deep night. We bloom
to redirect light from a day we can't
yet muster. Life uncorks another round.
We become the proprietors of one another's
checklists. We assume the forms of seatbelt,
mole-hill, tower. Be spider-silk, taut
across the vibration. We will pass
each atom. Someone else first imagined
the eternal. We clip our wicks, the universe grows.

(no subject)

I build glimmer and it turns
out to be as reckless as it sounds.
Every person I know does this too,
constructs that which is tangible
in one's apprehension.
A wand that helps me sleep and feed the life
of the brain which I hear
is an ever depreciating asset.
Or worse worth nothing like your testicles.
Worthless to science.

(no subject)

And yet we trickle into spaces as far out as is safe.
Sheered by distance, our names gradually sink
in the throats we were called by.
I tell myself not to count them.
Somehow, in spite of hard work at improvements,
the inner landscape never assembles sustainably.
Invite someone there. They see through the glass
you show them, a terrarium, that loses transparency.
I work to erect a hut in the woods knowing no craft.
There are two foundations from ruined cottages
to build on. I ask a friend to raise corner posts and mark
the door with a deer jaw. I want to say I'll finish
but it gets too hard. Eventually, it's filled in by snow.
I stay in the clearing. Around me, dry twigs crack
with blizzard. This was another dawn muffled by its accumulation.
I chain the wheels of our John Deere.
To get out of here, more than a bag of salt and a shovel are needed.

(no subject)

My friend I am sorry distance
is the ballad my guitar has been
waiting for maybe begging this tune
to come stupid as my fingers are not practice-bound
under an outside night's half-sheath
with which I'd thought I shared some vibration
or opportunity in a calamity but it was untrue
like most self-whispers I can't take back.
My car going over one hundred miles
per hour doesn't make the long highway
any shorter. The still-watching police cruiser
biding its time against the tide of the Bay's
high lonesome
plays its bellowing accordion.
But for the rowing of breath
I sustain what I take with me
out into the place I call the world and the world
calls the weather.
The hope of a moment
that stands apart from its birth.

(no subject)

It's cold, hot, and gracenote seasons
I am anxious to catch the slippage
maybe deep-fry a turkey. Hell, I'd fry about anything.
Pot's been harder to come by, so we spend
nights up in the barn, where the potential to do is uninsulated.
E's brought Black Label and his drums.
We're running tape. Nothing comes to us
but my sister is watching through her binoculars from the house.
His brother is back living with his mother.
The way we horseshoe around. Makes sense to light up
the present, all of it, is already on record. I go back
again and the barn is for sale. We keep it tidy this time
and enjoy the twilight comradery. Later, E turns over his Jeep's motor
and lets it down the hill. If it doesn't show up at home
he says, we can always dig it out tomorrow.

(no subject)

Once more following the encore
of another idea slipped into caffeine
and sliding in the way I've learned my senses
run and tangle with held-breath waiting
for the next self acceptance
which would be a superpower were it
what I possessed instead my curse
is quickness an adaptation just surface
enough to blend my inner able-ist above
he who paced his yard with a screwdriver
not knowing how to secure
his valley's shadow so it stays below
those peaks that whisper trust me
like a friend you don't know well enough
to say they'll answer the call you place
when you realize the remedy carried
its own consequence as you now carry your son
to daycare in shoes he's learning
to wear wordlessly and what now
will you do remembering your own.

(no subject)

Summer forgets the way young people
are supposed to grow old
sometimes spilling too much of themselves
into progressively deeper water
at this lake and me reflexively flinching
at its waves reflection infinitesimally small
from our cabin up the hill nothing
to impend a great evening
being given a water bottle for your birthday
we're all here I'm holding
a red plastic cup steady
like that country song "red solo cup"
there's no metaphor in it
there's no reception
out here where there is nothing anyway.

(no subject)

There's a storm about an hour south, whiteout.
Myself at the reins, even short jaunts between hosts get slippery.
I range the longer gaps on snow tires, keeping low
my gut's thoughts. I suppose I've put this distance in before
but not for mass, not as a formal half. When we collect
it's a new vocabulary of blood spoken between cooking shows.
We walk to a park through a land that barely qualifies as anything else.
It's actually comfortable to see myself learn stillness.
If I weren't, where would I go?
At the evening's service the answer is simple.
The priest stands afore a darkened fenestella.
Teenage girls in gothic makeup approach with a baby
that is real. The Nativity.

(no subject)

The ground is frozen and so we can't sink
the wrought iron fence which might keep the street
from the toddler and the lights hung
in the deepening dark which stretches colder
the longer I am here turning up the heat
and mixing Tom & Jerry's batter
with warm milk, rum, the sense that maybe
a break can be taken from the compulsive now
I spin on the world's tiniest gerbil wheel
even though I'm running out of want
the want waits for me
a hard conversation one seeks from their eyes
too red and yellow to play crystal ball
not less than
but I wondered as I made rock and roll
that bright day with my oldest friend
who will I lose who has already been lost the music
comes from sore fingers and the lesson
that shows my happiness is not
what I thought rather it is getting
what I don't want if
that something builds.

(no subject)

As light grows longer so does it shorten.
My old dog on the blacktop in the summer sun
knew the rhythm, the creek running under him
through a tunnel in the road. It was big enough to stand in
and on any number of days the neighborhood boys
would prowl to the edge, spearing for carp.
Once, I took the point of their spear through my top lip
but stopped it with a tooth. One dilemma can change the game.
The carp they killed had thick skin, like terracotta pottery.
Once you took one, by law you had to bury it.
I quarried a little hole myself. Bad eating, bottom-feeders.
If the dog found it, he'd cover his coat in the smell.

(no subject)

Evening corrals my private relationships
into a transitory sieve testing its threshold.
Soft wounds deploy in the gut's knobs
as certain facts stand vigil over circumstance.
Our faces gather and lug through the injury
but are too buried to reach surface level.
The invasion has no purpose except to fight
itself deeply and multiply. Encumbrance of being
grows stronger and presents its own face.
A vision in black night. How it stares
as we lay ourselves to the floor.
How could I have leapt through a life
with its light and tender banner?
I am waving my handkerchief
in recognition. The sudden annexation.
In return we are allowed a diminished plot
with no appetite to digest its azaleas.
We shape dirt walls against the next intruder.

(no subject)

Tonight I saw this big bird flat
on the interstate.
It's strange how I swerved
as if there were a difference in the carbon
and its internal mystery.
I know barely anything
about what's over my shoulder.
Why I peel my hangnails
back to see the raw self
as it makes me newer though it hurts.

(no subject)

It was the habitat that demanded
an answer but to realize I was capable
this young I went to someone else's summerhouse.
It's now been ten years
since my father nearly died
on my sister's birthday.
Survival can be a lonesome gift
but the will to drag it back is expressionless.
I put a sunburn on and tuck a little money
in my towel. These vacation nights
are propped up on stilts to ward
against breakage. With such precariousness
who would think Jimmy Buffet is a good idea?
Celibacy, sobriety, insomnia.
On vacation, the most rewarding arguments
are the ones you invent to avoid
everyone else.

(no subject)

I am in the meadow of my birth
the sweet grass is dry I am stepping
into it under autumn's heavy eyelids
above the dirt collected on a worn
traveler's coat its speckled fray a fuse
except actually invisible you see
there's no longer any place to get to
my life departed from itself
myself no lifeline just smooth palm
stretched as a road beyond my grasp
I want what can only be felt
if I let that through perhaps the daydream
would be a noon with natural light
filtering out the opaque ambiguities
of real life just the word inbox
a tightness in my DNA I can't
shake the river that runs through me
that drowns me with life so long as
I water it the right amount every day
so long as nothing gets in the way
around each other especially
when it shouldn't though sometimes
it should and maybe that's why
war exists the little war that's called

survival is an ambush
from the start.

(no subject)

I'm so dead, we used to say.
The uncertainty of self and choice
patched into vision, my struggle for sleep.
Even in a city, night is quiet enough to descend
into the flurry of one's own rhythms.
The walls are old plaster.
Tomorrow, I hope control will be tied
to a remission of little mendacities.
Our dog with its twisted bowels
will not be a problem. It will pass
or worsen, and that's okay. Slow it down.
A prophesy of left-turns is still a promise.

(no subject)

I've curated my dust into a pile
that signals the whole and helps the hour
pass. Resignation often dreams itself from afar.
When money finally dwindles, waiting grinds slower.
Tomorrow, I'll see dying. I'll shed the thought
and return to the charm that lies between my hands
bound by a rope so thin I can almost imagine it's not there.
The makers are floating by my window trailing
their little children as they thieve our twilight.
The landscape has changed, is always changing
but seems this time to have folded its igneous
away from my feet, as I tread forward
on its compressed-glass.

(no subject)

Afternoon picks a tender "so what"
from my daily correspondence.
As I slow my heartbeat, bees
sleepily clink against my window,
swarming over the ripe pears
dropped into the gutter by a tree
less than six feet away from the house
which apparently is the minimum distance
one plants their seeds from a foundation
as they are known to take root and grow
to break with their fruit and thirst
any surrounding structures as they rise
towards a midwest sky screened
and nearly subcutaneous against
western smoke blowing eastward,
a vengeance I perceive and which prompts me
to wonder, "when will I bug out?"
to that secret cabin I imagine lays a doormat
just for me to place all those talismans
I've kept within my chest, not overfilled
but unmanaged with its broken lighters
silver quarters, and keys all in a wet glint
that says "I know you though you've never

seen us together on the stoop,

but the door opens just beyond."

(no subject)

Our sleep's raw plume trailed in the sky
after the experience our friends had taken
to be with each other it's not time
that we expected to compact our
rituals that pass into the eye
and the through instant I take a Lyft back home
to my work though now it is raining again
the turbulence relegated above me
on a seat without walls.

(no subject)

Midnight cell signal dropped. Shouldn't bite tainted candy.
I hold my feverish reflection and never appear to change
my basic outlook but do want to talk with a bad mind
for details considering the implications of the front windows painted
shut on accident. Took a Buck knife 110 to them but came up worse
for wear and slipping in some old habits before shaking
out the dust and letting open the air. The neighbors have
been working on their place at odd hours and took electricity
direct from the line. I check the meter for energy I think I've
used myself, all while the dog hassles a couple walking past.
No big deal just haven't figured out how to keep things quiet
for extended time periods though without them I'd live
on top of myself, maybe go to more events but what's the point of that?
Each interaction a ghost summoned with uncommon complication
except who doesn't like free food and an opportunity
to talk about it or what else I imagine we find in common
or extraordinary. The jettisoned cargo and my radar blinking
on the screen in the dark with glare

(no subject)

That is to say I won't be calling you
to say what I've been thinking about
saying to you were I to pick up
the clothes I've tossed carelessly
beside the bed as I tuck into
another spasmodic thought that lingers
among the dark-room the black-out curtains
hung to keep from me the light
of night's growing brightness
getting larger every minute I've wasted
even still as my inability
to be still for you settles
into the figure in the painting
you envisioned desire and which
like many paintings was slapped
atop some already used canvas
too many colors layers markings and nowhere
notable enough to x-ray or excavate
and thus a new way of being simply comes
as it always has one half the picture intentioned
the other just brushstrokes under their cake
and breaking frame
which is probably a bit dramatic
but isn't that the point of learning

the arts anyway like how someone wrote
bats have it made.

(no subject)

My personal radar is scrambling
to tell me something about the air
in my lungs being that special
kind you find in your yard after midnight
that makes the small being lighter
just as I've wished to be
light for you.

(no subject)

Day rises over a silver C saxophone melody.
Among these early hours, there is an optimism for rain
but a preparation for HVAC. I skim my brain over
coffee's requisite molecular transfer. My commute
is a different type of motion. I absorb it.
On the way, I check my phone for text, a video
and my work just to be prepared. The day blooms slow
or quick. There's no more water cooler machine.
Dispatched for its expense. Conversations of money persist.
In the brashness of these loci, a justification of family
doesn't always jive with my basic humanist.
Even murderers believe they're doing the right thing.

(no subject)

It's easy to be tough
when what gets pulled
over another day is
the smell of drops
that naturally fall in grass
patches I'd sleep by
imagining my tracks
as an alien rope
knotted with age I should
no longer be
allowed what's not deep
sleep I'm after
the idea of how
others see me anyway
clouded behind the quartz
membrane of
if I'd had enough
rest I'd be there though
who knows.

(no subject)

Windlands stratify into a state of Wisconsin.
It must be fall. When jostling compounds, I am sick
in the back of the station wagon. We stop in a bar
that commemorates Houdini. Our progress slows.
Cosmic American music is the last check of my close familiar
as we enter this particular cradle. At the homestead
I am given a ten-volume set of books that belonged
to my great-great-aunt, who worked for city hall in, I think, the 30's.
The universe, I read, was not built by sheer force
but adhered to laws it was born into. I try to believe what I can.
A different shading in the word law. Later, we make for the river
where I watch the water until the first keeper spasms forth.
I can feel it through my arms. I'm educated on the proper clean
and toss my shirt on a dead branch.

(no subject)

The week grows quickly as my son
has learned to fill his crib
with the broken stems of lilies
I planted for him
in our garden. Outside
the wind is moving faster
the window loose in its frame simultaneously
banging and howling with the dog
at the mail carrier whose package
drops from her gloves
and lays just beyond the shadow
of my front stoop roof. Quiet
and impassable to air
that moves around it. A new interval
differentiated by a pitch my ear
tries to sort from other sounds
into some illusion of linearity
under which lies another
microtone I know
must be the note
I've never heard
I haven't learned
how to receive.

(no subject)

Point to a chaos I remember
as the picture drawn in my eye
before I learned that thinking differently
doesn't make anything happen
just helps me fill my glove with lead
and isn't that something
everyone wants but why it sometimes
feels harsher than this hope.
When I was three I asked my dad
will grandpa die will grandma will ray
will mom will you will what soil makes
of this kaleidoscope feel like anything
other than light escaping from a faraway sun's
dark ellipsis this summery April evening
carried by a lamp that's flickering
ridiculously. There's no time
to fix it tonight let's draw a bath or slip
in some online retail therapy.

(no subject)

I was stalked. Fluxed eyesight on stone.
Under every clownish step, the gristle.
Blent pastels drum a burst of California Bay Laurels.
Outside, particulates escape.
Sun excitement on every side of the Bay is skeletal or asleep.
Under death it heaps itself up higher.
Dilemmas modulate a constant combination
of history and fishing. The riggings are a mess.
Ground covered, shale covered, sky covered.
Ill-fated saucers of industry's milk.
I thought I was asleep.
I believed it.
There are past lives inside a wooden pencil.
The sun was risen by then
muscling air between two stones.
Afraid of the cliff, by the edge, concrete grew rusty.
Everything in earthen colors and leaking.

(no subject)

Window spider rearranges what
I know, the fissure between now and
after I grabbed a cup and a tissue.
I live with what I've done to another
number I put myself into.
Today black coffee
is for fathers. I donated
online because my separations are
only a call away.
We hear each other's moments.
I admit I can't get stoned anymore.
My parking ticket went to collections.
As it turns, sex is basic life
but unlike basic sex life is a world
so one's never finished.

(no subject)

There is no left left to say
no book to rip a page from and fold
into the creek's cool stream
through the green particulate toward
no inlet no place to outpour into
and lay with the weight of big water
over you looking upward toward
no sky no brim for this world
no moon in orbit past yourself
no knowledge of the natural satellite itself
as no good for material in your not yet realized clutch
of words not yet born nor unborn
in an act of what you feel not quite
as blame excuse just the feeling of one blue
life and another passing rabbit
outside your window eating a spring
tulip as you wonder what's not wrong
with this equation the potential
of a brain with too many creases
folding over on themselves to shrink
the surface area with each tuck
no drive to amalgamate
instead just like cutting a pizza in half
and in half and in half and in half

and in half and in half and so on.
Eventually there's no pizza left
just some atomic trace as the lingering
ghost of a pepperoni.

(no subject)

It's difficult to write what lies
perfectly writes itself your life
can sense its siren vibrate deep
but your feeling can't detect changes
of pressure in the surrounding
medium through time through
such an organ I've made myself
some tea which I never drink
unless I'm out of coffee today
is Sunday and I've taken a conference
call am going to a pool party
however I don't want to I'm behind
the house and playing fetch
my toes are open and cold
on the flagstone I need to call
the family later my Dad sent a video
of his dog laying in the creek
a house is a special kind of box I spend
my time in though I guess what adds up
is always some kind of container
punctuated by the vastness
of the packaging.

(no subject)

I exercise Echo beyond the neighbors' pastel stucco
and am similarly peeled back by the sun.
My East Bay outdoors are a throughway
between differently shaped tables. I like it here
and that can make me feel stupid.
That I too have become a sitter whose circulatory
keeps me moving, even recovering, when necessary.
Extending a palm to be read, I discover what will come
isn't what I predicted, but could be worse.
A hopeful possession by phantom self.
Like the time I encountered a bear
rummaging trash along a country street
and realized I shouldn't take its picture. I had already
chosen poorly and ran.

(no subject)

In fact no bend has been here
though sunlight sometimes makes
a shell of heart's geode
reflecting in my eye the tear becomes another
reaction older than speech but what hasn't
been already coopted by human epiphany
I left my car light on it killed the battery
isn't supposed to make a dent however I
realize that I can't illuminate this fate
for where my clothes may have fallen they felt
less hidden than lost every road has a ditch
and it's time I ran into one
to see why I need the windows open
when I sleep and why I like
to let it in so much.

(no subject)

I saw you dribble wine
on the white sofa
and didn't fetch any soda.
It becomes harder to feel angry.
Every day, I sit in the same position
and fret to look composed.
Molecules in constant movement.
The delight of a cheap deli sandwich.
I close my eyes.
I'm a Midwesterner and private
so sometimes it is difficult
to demonstrate locate affection.

(no subject)

I was surprised to find skylight's brush
spreading the day out. I woke up late
gathered my wits without taking a shower.
I started remembering the night before.
Trying to stay true to someone who told me he's proof
anyone can change but the carnations I was gifted
are dying already the water keeps getting greener
and I haven't had time to change
it before leaving to meet my coworker super hung-over
though I hid it pretty well. Picked up a rental van
with the damage waiver and took it to a dead woman's house
where I laid claim to her midcentury cabinetry and maybe
a bedroom set except the family wants to keep it together.
I haven't quite got room but could secretly break it up.
Everyone I know needs a new dresser and is sick
of the prices Urban Ore tries to charge. Drinking water
and coconut juice. Rehydrate while I consider the cost
of daycare the cost of living keeps going up and I'm trying
to find a deal on someone who can reupholster a lounge chair
and ottoman I also was able to bring home because it's stained
but stable and I'd like to put my feet up.

(no subject)

What is the point I ask out loud.
The form of the question itself an emptying
into space from a place that can't offer any scrutiny.
The negative of a small geometric painting
my friend gave me and I hung
behind the dining table. Five black squares
on grey paneling quite possibly a kitten's face
though my friend later adopted a puppy
that is loveable and badly behaved
in the gentle sort of way. I often felt
badly behaved though it's lesser with age.
Exercise discipline & praise in that order.
My own dog's trainer told me to focus..
I stare at a monitor with too many windows open
alongside the thought that maybe I can't
do a task that would only take two minutes.
I'm thirsty, eating my child's goldfish
crackers calling my wife to see what time she'll be done.
The sky slightly darkens though the January fringe
seems almost lumed and hungry for the smallest
plate of light it might reflect and I might utilize
to find the peephole of my own front door
squinting through it with hands pressed up
though my fingers and toes are numb
from some form of exposure that comes

no matter how long I keep myself
inside and waiting.

(no subject)

Under this fluorescent
night's corners there is no
other face to see me
straighten therefore
hear my gray breath
woven by a trick
of mind's faux silence
turning up the tune
as if more of what was added
yesterday is not the day before
I fossilized or whatever
happens when what's inside
is finally exchanged
for stone.

(no subject)

Feeling blue about
the basement carried above
my core I said I want to trade
in my way of doing
used to be simpler fitting
things together these days
it's hard since one
maybe two or three
fingers hide behind my
shush I'm home later than
I expect and quiet in spring's
not so subtle umbrella.

(no subject)

Why is it some memories rise
while others lilt unrecognizably
into the seasoning of our framework.
I enter my familiar places and am surprised
at how my touch is reencountered.
Try not to think about it.
Today the sky is blue as ever it was
when I was light with the hollow bones
of boyhood. Like when our family
field burned a few years ago.
What was once destroyed
is green today.

(no subject)

Here's how to attack: machines, clover
atomized registers of weight weeping
through the mouth, provide more meat
in the after-the-fact song, push towards a local pride
the fleshly mirror with some sound of voice.
Hear my own voice differently.
Wasps wield their poison.
Chase the chasm back from the busted play.
An alternate dream survived in tape.
The sequoia echoes.
Autumn nailed to the overpass.

(no subject)

Noticing that in doing nothing what I've done
is bite my thumb-nail below the callous.
Sitting in the open the chalky flesh burns unevenly in the quiet.
Home is shrouded in the sleep of others. My own
stillness is a treaty with each aspiration. How many
keystrokes will it take to capture the feeling?
I hold behind the latched gate too much anxiety.
I feel more than stripped naked which is inherently
a danger to any living being.

(no subject)

I live for what I wrote
after I discovered life
is undergraduate mixed media
hung in my home as I listen
to the toilet run from day to day
tasks I told myself I had to address
which is why we kept
the puppy even after she made
our trainer bleed I thought
I love to look in eyes
so coal you can't tell what
will happen though I can
only learn impossibility
through the act of trying
to clean off my desk.

(no subject)

Lend me your flute
while I search the table.
I have no eyes for instinct or craft.
I smell smoke from the chimney
of the outpost where they are known
to meet. I drag myself there upon a crutch
of snapped twigs. Like some others
my ivory horn is a sprout of celebrations
that glimmers against the dirt when I dig
out my bed. Every night I need sleep.
Sometimes I find in that slumber an egg
which I cradle.

(no subject)

How far does the light go to turn
its color
the shade of my dog
now middle-aged sleeping
on the floor under the window
beyond which the street runs
throughout the day.
The road is windowless.
Am I to see past it?
I am dark-suited in my work
which is necessary
among the plant-beds.
What is that flower that's opened
by ants? Peonies.
The natural fat of the season
rising and enfolding my senses.
Is it any wonder I am just a pebble
to this world? I've been trying
to talk with nobody.
I wanted to be effaced.
my heart is a cardboard box
I'm too tired to carry up the stairs.

(no subject)

This scrape opens
still-life to materials
that always surprised me.
Vesicles of meaning
through proximity
seep a plain me
I swear I'd memorized.

epilogue(s)

(i)

The blinds are drawn
in this room built for sun.
Light struggles through
in its little slant making visible
the room's particulates around me,
entering my body and breath,
as a barely perceptible periphery
of my existence in this home.

(ii)

I'd like to tell you something
impressive. I'm spending
my whole day trying to amplify it
but am struggling to carry
a thought out of repetition's mirror
before it cracks.

(iii)

Downstairs a handyman is at work
building an Ikea daybed
for a soon coming guest.
I thought I could do it,
but I needed help. Have you
ever taken a pill for something
like that? I've taken everything
I can imagine for happiness,
except what another might
prescribe.

(iv)

I'm on a health kick.
I ate four eggs for breakfast.
I will eat four oz of turkey at lunch.
Today I'm skipping gym day.
I'm skipping work. I'm sitting
at my computer completely alone,
which is a treat I rarely give myself,
and struggle to digest.

(v)

What use is the solitude
I've told myself I need?
Here I am typing into what is only
the widening space I've put between
myself and who I pictured I'd become.
The past two years have been
commonly uncommon, so let's get that
out of the way. The worst parts
have dread's cliché-cobweb clinging
to them as I try to write them down,
and the best surprise me as I find
on my page untendered language,
the unexpectedly unintended that drips
with what I didn't know I knew.

(vi)

I almost never leave home.
None of us do. Don't talk, don't walk,
too cold these last few months,
though summer is painted
on our front door's concrete slab.

(vii)

I will be the last to hear
my five-month-old giggle.
I wait for changes tied to the season.
For those things that haven't changed,
I decided to see a therapist
for the first time in my life.

(viii)

I can't talk about this through metaphor,
where it's too easy to numb myself.
My counselor started our first session
with the family tree. Outside
my still drawn window,
there is an actual willow tree
with a broken bough dangling.

(ix)

Sorry to put it this way but it cracks
me up how presence works.
It's not the branch that I perceive,
it's the dangling task of trimming.
I need a taller ladder, and mentally
going up it reminds me I need to call
my grandparents, who just had a fall
on the escalator at Menards.

(x)

Where my grandparents fell
was that kind of escalator that also locks
your shopping carts to the rail
as you descend. So they got run over
by the cart behind them and somehow
are ok. They are ninety
and I tell myself that I do things
I shouldn't all the time.

(xi)

The handyman just let me know
he's leaving. A bigger client called
and he can maybe put in some time tomorrow.
Tomorrow, I'll make up my gym day.
Almost every day I work in the bright-dark
of this same office. I struggle
to explain what I do.

(xii)

My therapist observed
I manage a lot of egos and that is true
professionally speaking. To manage
or be managed. I haven't told her yet about how
at around 12 years old I tried to lay in the frozen creek
to give myself hypothermia. I don't remember why,
but it had to do with my liar's emotions.

(xiii)

I am a practitioner
of the occasionally fucked art
of keeping others happy.
I walked dripping back home,
and got laughed at as the child I was.
Right now I'm running a fan
on the interior carpet of my 1993 Toyota.
It too is wet and I have no idea
how it happened.

(xiv)

I believe in the aura of the object.
I am surrounded by the enchanted
and the half-broken. My Toyota leaks oil
on the driveway. I try to see possibility
in inconvenience and sometimes succeed.

(xv)

To be able to follow intuition
to the discovery of, say, a pair
of 210-year-old Redouté stipple prints
in the corner of the thrift store.
It is tempting to say to myself it's good,
it's honorable, that I am a fixer
since that is how much of my time is spent,
but what I want is for myself;
a life of acts of quickened-pulse,
of thrill-ride suspense.

(xvi)

How to fix myself is the question
I can type but will any phrase fix
my need to ask? When I was a child,
I believed I could make my hand levitate
by flexing all the little muscles
and letting it hover above a flat surface.
Now my pinky and my thumbs
get sore as I type. Repetitive motion.
Which would be a good band name,
if I had a band to name.

(xvii)

Tonight, I'll be cooking dinner.
In the household distribution of labor,
I do the cooking. Call it "Chez Daddy,"
though my three-year-old never eats what I make.
He doesn't get that from me but in him
I still see myself. There are two versions:
one belongs to him and the other
is my small me I still talk to in my sleep.

(xviii)

As a parent, maybe Larkin got it half right
since my children fuck me up.
Who am I to complain? For years
I've been thinking about how to write
about my diagnosis. In my 30s I learned
the term I hesitate to use.
I don't want it to be public, processed.
Rote, verbal, audio.

(xix)

For my operating system's lack
of a manual, I beg poetry's shadowy cloak
to conceal the words above. I need to find
the true metaphor, and then delete the cliché
of "shadowy cloak." Which is ridiculous.
Who are all the people I think will read this poem
and how can I imagine what they want?

(xx)

We are, to quote the professor
who wouldn't publish me,
experiencing late-stage capitalism.
Which apparently is also a good excuse
to make out with your students.
That economy is why I left Bay Area
fog and fire for a simpler
micropolitan life.

(xxi)

When will I return to the Bay? I miss the people
and the poets. Sometimes they're the same thing.
But here in South Dakota our house is large,
our dog is happy. Outside the city limits,
I shoot clay discs with a shotgun
until my shoulder hurts.
The proprietor asks me,
"alone again?"

(xxii)

Daily I withdraw and paint myself
with my home as a shellac
against feeling. I wish to be fondly
regarded which sometimes means
not saying anything.

(xxiii)

Years ago I took a swipe at professor-culture
on another poet's Facebook page.
They felt I minimized their initial complaint
and I felt horrible until more recently
I discovered they're a vaccine denier,
so fuck 'em. Maybe that's an unhealthy outlook
I've adopted to let myself off easily.

(xxiv)

When my wife and I were drinking more
we'd argue. The real fight is to embrace
and cultivate my more angelic impulses.
How can I find the voice of fate
in the dishes I forgot to wash?

(xxv)

My son wakes up and sometimes
the first thing he says is "I don't want you"
which I know he doesn't mean.
He means he wants his mother,
in his limited vocabulary of choice.
We're all unrepentant sociopaths
as children, and my son also happens
not to be a morning person, which I admit,
I'm not either.

(xxvi)

Take this next bit with a grain
of your preferred spice. I'm about to talk
about the poem again. The stage curtains
rustling around the day I plod through,
a few hundred words stretched
around not just "the day," which is every day,
but what might extend beyond all the
expanse of days. Maybe the poem stretches
me to see beyond them. Can readers share that,
depending on how I write these lines?

(xxvii)

Last night, outside my mother-in-law's window
the summer's first hummingbird came
for a drink of sugar water.
It was Arlene's night to cook,
which is always infused with seasonings
you can't pull from a Hy-Vee recipe book.

(xviii)

While I'm on this health regime
I've been trying to find new nourishment.
My biggest problem is impulse control.
After the last time I was sick I procrastinated
getting a blood test. I don't want to understand
my illness, just want to be cured.
I'm ready with my copay.

(xxix)

I complain about the term "late-stage capitalism,"
even though I pretty much agree with it
and sympathize with the symptoms.
All my life I've wished to live and love doing it.
To run with my kids through the gates
of summer's first soft hint. Which is a hell
of a privilege, as I sit in this house
that I own with the help of a bank,
on stolen indigenous land, a debt
I have done little to repay.

(xxx)

I recently received a massage
from Sioux Falls' only blind masseuse,
and as he brought my left shoulder
2" from below my right, he talked
about his red Mustang convertible.
700 horsepower with a carbon fiber hood,
and named Sasha after his favorite porn-star.
He said he wished that he could drive it,
but now only his daughter can.
I left with some questions and a body
in that liminal state between
broken and fixed.

(xxxi)

I feel like I'm coming
out of a coma. What else is there to do
but accept that the poem moves
a lot slower than my life. Yet the meaning
of my life has to wait a long time
to be found in my poem. I wrote
one hundred pages over ten years.

(xxxii)

Since my last line of poetry was written,
another box has been checked
on my family's health chart, as we wait
for an afternoon tornado that never
touches down. We are sitting together
in the basement watching Mickey Mouse.

(xxxiii)

These days, all I'm left to do is wonder.
I'm trying to watch how I talk
about it and remember to look forward.
Sometimes I sense what is pushing
through my callouses—
those little happy pokes, which pin me
to a sense of living, and that I feel a bit
bad about, as if nothing is ever enough.
Who am I to need a jolt?

(xxxiv)

Through the wall I'm listening
to my sick young boy cry to his mother.
We have an airline that won't refund
our money. My son's sudden serious illness
doesn't matter to American.
I wish I could make them feel
what he says is in his bones.

(xxxv)

I'm waiting to finish out
another workday, on this national holiday
built to memorialize, which I read
comes from the word memoria
meaning simply memory.
I think it's almost impossible
to share a memory. I suspect
it's easier to share a fantasy,
but that's probably a fantasy in itself.

(xxxvi)

My wife has little memory
of my son being born, though I recall
the sound she made as the doctors
traced their incision in the gauzy shield
of her kinked epidural. All's well that ends
with a baby in your arms. Everything
in my arms that I allow burble
into this poem is most alive
if I give it away.

Acknowledgements

Some of these poems have appeared in *Dispatches from the Poetry War*, *Witness: A Magazine of the Black Mountain Institute*, *Tammy*, *The Offending Adam*, *The Laurel Review*, and *White Stag*, as well as the chapbook *Cosmic American Music*, published by Old Gold in 2017.

Thanks first and foremost to Nicole for her support, and her patience for all those times I came home too late after hanging out with the poets.

This book is dedicated to my friends and colleagues at speCt, Gillian Olivia Blythe Hamel, Robert Andrew Perez, and Chris Philpot, who have been my poetry siblings and without whom I couldn't have completed this work.

I also want to thank all of the poets who helped me generate work through the University Press Books Writing Workshops, and all of its subsequent iterations. Thank you to my peers at the SMC MFA.

Thank yous also go to Cedar Sigo, who believed in me and published my first chapbook, Jamie Townsend for their help editing this manuscript, and the influential teachers I've had over the years: Shannon Hannigan, John Colburn, Nick Regiacorte, Monica Berlin, Graham Foust, Brenda Hillman, Dora Malech, Shane Book, David Lau, and Chris Sindt, among many others.

Thank you to the poets and publishers who have inspired me over the years, who are too innumerable to count.

And last but not least, thank you to Rusty Morrison, not just for your talent as the greatest living poetry editor in North America, but for your mentorship, friendship, and wisdom.

Peter Burghardt is a writer who spends his time in the Midwest and the SF Bay Area. He co-founded and edits speCt books with Gillian Olivia Blythe Hamel, Robert Andrew Perez, and Chris Philpot. His work has appeared in various magazines and journals online and in print. His chapbook, Cosmic American Music, is available from Old Gold Press.

photo by Robert Andrew Perez

(no subject)
by Peter Burghardt

Cover art by Marion Kryczka

Interior typefaces: Garamond and Futura.

Cover design by Peter Burghardt
Interior design by Laura Joakimson

Printed in the United States
by Books International, Dulles, Virginia
On 55# Glatfelter B19 Antique 360 ppi
(for books over 100 pages use:) On Glatfelter 50# Cream Natures Book 440 ppi
Acid Free Archival Quality Recycled Paper

Publication of this book was made possible in part by gifts from
Katherine & John Gravendyk in honor of Hillary Gravendyk,
Francesca Bell, Mary Mackey, and The New Place Fund

Omnidawn Publishing
Oakland, California
Staff and Volunteers, Spring 2022

Rusty Morrison & Ken Keegan, senior editors & co-publishers
Laura Joakimson, production editor and poetry & fiction editor
Rob Hendricks, editor for *Omniverse*, poetry & fiction, & post-pub marketing,
Sharon Zetter, poetry editor & book designer
Jeff Kingman, copy editor
Liza Flum, poetry editor
Anthony Cody, poetry editor
Jason Bayani, poetry editor
Gail Aronson, fiction editor
Jennifer Metsker, marketing assistant
Jordyn MacKenzie, marketing assistant
Sophia Carr, marketing assistant